K

MW01291477

Cancer

Analysis and Understanding of Ketosis as a Complementary Nutrition-Based Cancer Therapy

By

Jamie Knight

Table of Contents

Introduction

How are cancer and ketogenic diets related? How can a fat-based keto diet help in controlling the growth and spread of tumor cells? I hope I can answer these and more questions on the said subject. We start with the basic understanding of cancer and how it spreads. Some of the terms mentioned in this section are used in the other sections of this book; therefore, it is important to get a basic idea of cancer and its effects.

What is Cancer?

Cells are the fundamental units of the human body. Old and damaged cells are replaced by new cells that are formed through the process of cell division. New cells are formed as and when the body needs them. It is a very orderly process.

When this orderly process is disrupted through known or unknown means, the following things take place:

- There is an uncontrollable growth of cells.
- These cells may form a tumor; benign or malignant (or cancerous).
- Benign tumors do not spread, whereas malignant tumors can spread.
- Some kinds of cancers such as myeloma, leukemia, and a few types of lymphoma do not form tumors.

Types of Cancers

Cancers are divided into four main types including:

Carcinomas

This kind of cancer starts off either in the skin or the outer covering of internal glands and organs. There is usually a presence of a solid tumor in this kind of cancer. The common examples of carcinomas are breast cancer, prostate cancer, colorectal cancer, and lung cancer.

Sarcomas

This type of cancer begins in the supporting and connective tissues of the body, such as muscles, fat, tendons, nerves, blood vessels, joints, bone or cartilage, and lymph vessels.

Leukemia

This is a cancer of the blood and begins when healthy blood cells grow and alter uncontrollably.

Lymphoma

This type of cancer starts in the lymphatic system which is a network of glands and vessels that help in fighting infections.

The Spread of Cancer

As cancerous tumors grow, the lymphatic system, or the bloodstream, can carry the cancer cells to the other parts of the body. This process is referred to as metastasis. During the process of metastasis, the cancer cells may grow further and also develop into new cancer cells. One of the most common places that cancer spreads is the lymph nodes, the bean-shaped organs that help in fighting infection. Clusters of lymph nodes are found in different parts of the body, such as the underarms, the groin area, and the neck. Cancers also spread via the bloodstream to affect even distant parts of the body, such as bones, lungs, brain, liver, etc.

Even when the cancer spreads to other parts of the body, the name that is used to refer to it is that area where it began. For example, if a carcinoma originating in the breast (breast cancer) spreads to the lungs, it is referred to as metastatic breast cancer and is not called lung cancer.

While some people recognize unusual symptoms which are then connected to cancer by the doctor during diagnoses, there are many people who exhibit no symptoms whatsoever of cancer. Many times cancer is diagnosed when the person visits the doctor to get treatment for some other disease or health issue. That is how mysteriously cancer works!

Chapter 1: The Working of Ketogenic Metabolism Triggered by Low Carb, Fat-Burning Diets

Referred to by many other names including ketogenic diet, low-carb-high-fat (LCHF) diet, and low carb diet, a keto diet involves the consumption of primarily fat with lower proportions of proteins and carbs. In a keto diet, your liver produces ketones which are used as the primary source of energy instead of glucose. Let us understand how a carb diet works first.

How a Carb Diet Works

When you eat carbohydrates, your body produces glucose along with insulin. For the human body, glucose is the easiest molecule to convert into its energy source so it will choose glucose over any other source of energy. Insulin is needed by the body to process glucose and transfer the produced energy to other parts of the body through the bloodstream.

Now, as glucose is being used for energy, the other energy sources, such as fats and proteins, are not used for this purpose and get accumulated and stored in the body. In a carb-rich diet, glucose is the only molecule used as energy fuel as it is abundantly available in the body.

How a Keto Diet Works

In a keto diet, you are reducing the intake of carbs, thereby compelling your body to choose other energy molecules for its fuel. Lowering carb intake takes your body into a ketosis state, a natural survival mechanism of the body. During the ketosis state, the liver produces ketones by breaking down fat molecules. The final aim of a well-balanced and well-planned keto diet is to change the metabolic state of your body permanently to ketosis from glucose metabolism.

A keto diet makes this happen, not by starving the body of food entirely, but starving it of carbohydrates, thereby forcing ketosis to take place. Our body is incredibly adaptive and can change depending on what you feed it with. If you starve your body of carbohydrates, it can easily change its primary fuel source to fats and get into ketosis.

There are multiple benefits of following a keto diet including weight loss, increased energy levels, and the prevention and control of many diseases including cancer

the primary focus of this book. Before going into the details of the various benefits of a keto diet, let us look how keto diets help in giving you these benefits.

The Cellular Perspective

To recap, glucose is the body's preferred source of energy. When the body is starved of this source, it automatically searches for other energy sources and one of them is ketosis or the breaking down of fats to form ketones, an alternative to glucose. These ketones can be used by all cells for their energy requirement; yet, there are many differences in the way ketone bodies and glucose molecules work to provide the required energy.

For example, when glucose is burned for fuel, a lot of reactive oxygen is released. Excessive levels of reactive oxygen can damage cells, cause inflammation, and even result in cell death; therefore, excessive sugar consumption is one of the primary reasons attributed to brain function impairment and plaque formation in the brain.

Ketones, on the other hand, are known to be efficient sources of energy and even help in protecting neuron cells of the brain. When ketones are broken down for energy needs, the production of reactive oxygen is reduced in addition to improved production and functioning of mitochondria.

When ketones become the main fuel source instead of glucose, even the struggling unhealthy cells get a boost of health because of the absence of reactive oxygen.

When carbs are not sufficiently available to the cell, it goes into a state of autophagy, which increases overall cell health and its resilience. The autophagy process also helps in cleaning up damaged cells and retarding anti-inflammatory processes.

It is this combination of ketone burning (for fuel) and improved autophagy that is believed to be the reason for keto diets to be effective treatments for cancer and brain damage diseases, such as Alzheimer's, epilepsy, and migraines.

The Body Perspective

When the body is starved of carbs, the biggest stimulator for the production and release of insulin is restricted resulting in decreased levels of insulin in the bloodstream. The decreased level of insulin triggers the following three important changes in the body:

- Increased burning of fat
- Reduction of inflammation

Decreased consumption of carbs, therefore, curbs three important drivers of chronic diseases; inflammation, fat accumulation, and insulin resistance, thereby helping in improved health.

More about Ketones and Ketosis

If you look at the diet our cavemen subsisted on, it was mainly fat-based. Ketones were the primary source of fuel for the human body for thousands of years before glucose was discovered. Moreover, our ancestors did not get access to food for long periods of time as hunting and gathering took a lot of time and effort. Subsisting on fat sources proved to be very beneficial during the periods when food was scarce as high-fat diets are very satiating and one doesn't feel hungry for a long time.

Type of Ketones

Ketones or ketone bodies are formed when fatty acids are broken down in the liver. There are primarily three kinds of ketones released in the body, including:

- Acetoacetate (AcAc)
- Beta-hydroxybutyric acid (BHB)
- Acetone

The first two types of ketones are responsible for transporting energy to the other parts of the body. Acetoacetate is the first type of ketone body that is formed during the process of ketosis which is used to form Beta-hydroxybutyric acid (BHB). Acetone is a by-product formed during the production of acetoacetate. Acetone is the least used ketone in the human body. If acetone is not used soon after production, then it is broken down and eliminated from the body, either through the urine or via the breath. Acetone gives the fruity smell to breath when a person is in a ketosis state.

While it has multiple general benefits for users, including the obvious weight loss advantage, a well-balanced keto diet is also proven to curtail the onset and spread of certain specific health disorders, including diabetes, vascular diseases, Alzheimer's, and more. With this in mind, I have divided the benefits into two segments

the general benefits and the advantages targeted at specific disorders.

General Benefits of Keto Diets

Weight Loss

Many studies have proven that the primary cause of weight gain is a carbohydrate-rich diet which stimulates the production of insulin. When carbs are consumed, the pancreas releases insulin into the bloodstream. Insulin is needed to break down glucose for energy.

Additionally, insulin interferes with fat cells preventing them from being used as fuel for energy. This results in fat being accumulated and stored in the body, resulting in weight gain. Starving the body of carbohydrates prevents the release of insulin, thereby freeing up fat cells for use in the energy requirements of the body. Reduction of fat accumulation automatically results in weight loss.

Improved Brain Functioning

Keto diets restrict carb intake and increase the release of ketones for energy, resulting in the following three effects of brain functioning:

- Reduced inflammation
- Increased efficiency of brain cells
- Activation of health-inducing neurotrophic factors

Ketones are specifically effective for the effective balancing of Gamma-Amino Butyric Acid (GABA) and glutamate, which are important neurotransmitters in the brain. How do ketones help in this regard? Here is a simple explanation-

while glutamate is a stimulating neurotransmitter, GABA is an important inhibitory neurotransmitter. The balancing of these two elements helps in improved functioning of the brain.

Glutamic acid and glutamate are important ingredients for the production of GABA. If your brain uses up glutamic acid and glutamate as primary fuels, then there will not be enough left to convert into GABA, resulting in reduced levels of GABA as against the levels of the glutamate. This unbalanced situation results in a lack of focus and brain fog.

When the brain gets another energy source in the form of ketones, the glutamate is then free for conversion to GABA, resulting in a more balanced GABA-glutamate combination needed for efficient brain function. Moreover, GABA is proven to reduce stress and anxiety as well.

Increased Energy Levels

Keto diets are proven to improve mitochondrial function while reducing the production of highly reactive oxygen. Improved functioning of cellular mitochondria translates to increased energy levels in the cells. This situation, combined with reduced levels of reactive oxygen in the cells, results in improved energy efficiency in the body; therefore, a keto diet empowers you to get optimum energy from the food you eat resulting in an improved quality of life.

Decreased Inflammation

Keto diets reduce the levels of reactive oxygen which, in turn, reduces cell damage; therefore, the body's inflammatory processes don't have to be repeatedly brought in to do damage-recovery work, thereby decreasing the overall inflammation levels. People suffering from chronic pain-related diseases could notice a reduction in their pain too.

Benefits of Keto Diets for Specific Disorders

For Epilepsy

Way back in 1924, Dr. Russell Wilder of the famous Mayo Clinic, prescribed and designed a low-carb diet for children with epilepsy. At that time, the observations showed a considerable decrease in the seizure incidents among the participants. However, the first published study of the effect of keto diets on treating epilepsy took place in 1998 when 150 epileptic children were recruited for the program. Despite being on anti-seizure medication, these children had more than two seizures a week.

During the one-year trial period, these children were prescribed with keto diets. About three months later, nearly 34% of the children reported a reduced number of seizures (nearly 90% reduction). Only 71% of the children remained on the keto diet even after six months. About 32% now had 90% fewer seizures. At the end of the year, only 55% of the children remained on the diet and 27% reported that their incidence of seizures was reduced by 90%.

From this study, researchers concluded that keto diets complemented by anti-seizure medicines were a better form of treating epilepsy than by medication alone. More such studies have been conducted with the same results.

For Type-2 Diabetes

There have been ample studies which have proven that a carb-controlled diet regulates the insulin level in the bloodstream more effectively than a carb-rich diet. These studies discovered a clear connection between the level of insulin in the blood and the restriction of carbohydrates. Keto diets are effective complementary measures to treat Type-2 diabetes.

For Blood Pressure

Studies conducted by various researchers independently have proven that low-carb diets are the best way to treat blood pressure (complemented with medications) as compared to other kinds of diets; therefore, a low-carb diet is seen to be more effective than a low-fat diet to counter and control blood pressure.

For Alzheimer's Disease

Most studies on Alzheimer's have observed one common thing and that is the excessive intake of sugar impairs brain function and facilitates plaque build-up. Many experiments involving the use of ketone supplements have proven that brain functioning does show a significant improvement. Scientists gave MCT oil (found abundantly in coconut oil) to patients suffering from Alzheimer's and they noticed that these patients experienced a better recall capacity than before. Other benefits of ketones on brain health are:

- Prevention of neuronal loss
- Preservation of neuronal function
- Protection of brain cells from injury

In addition to the above, studies on ketogenic diets have proven that they help in treating and managing heart diseases, increasing the level of good cholesterol, and also in the treatment of infertility and polycystic ovary syndrome in women. More studies have also shown the effectiveness of ketogenic diets as a complementary therapy for the treatment of non-alcoholic liver diseases that are connected to obesity, type-2 diabetes, and heart diseases. Keto diets are also known to help in reducing the intensity of and preventing migraines.

And finally, keto diets are found to be very effective as complementary therapies for the treatment of cancer. Following a keto diet, along with the intake of conventional drugs and medicines, have proven to help in cancer remission. In fact, there are case studies wherein patients have reported a progression in their cancer when they stopped following keto diets.

More about the last one in the rest of the book.

Chapter 2: The Deep Connection between Cancer, Ketosis, and Mitochondrial Therapy

There are multiple answers that are needed to find cures and solutions to the mind-boggling disease called cancer. While a complete and unequivocal cure for cancer is not immediately in the offing, the good news is if diagnosed early, it is highly possible to control its spread through a combination of prescribed medications, diets, and other factors.

Thanks to continuous research work conducted by many medical universities and research centers all over the world, the global medical team is unraveling layers of this complex disease. Through the process of unraveling, new clues are being discovered. These revealing clues are helping medical professionals find ways and methods to help prevent cancerous cells from developing and spreading. These ways and methods combine lifestyle changes, dietary changes, and targeted cancer therapies in the form of conventional and new-found drugs and chemo.

One particularly interesting development in this regard is the interest shown by medical professionals and research scientists to the connection between cancer and ketogenic diets. The oncology and research communities of the world are increasing the momentum in this field, driven by interesting and promising observations recorded in studies connecting keto diets and cancer. Scientists and doctors agree that there are many cancers that are very responsive to certain dietary changes.

Cancer So Far

What do we know about cancer so far? There are more than 100 types of cancers documented; out of which, the five most common ones are breast, lung, stomach, colorectal, and prostate cancers. The common element of all types of cancers is uncontrolled cell growth. Here are some typical activities of cancer cells.

- Cancer cells avoid programmed cell death referred to as apoptosis. In contrast to necrosis (a process in which there is unregulated digestion of the components of cells), apoptosis is a programmed and natural way to eliminate damaged and old cells to be replaced by healthy and new cells.

- Cancer cells decrease their resistance to expand, grow, and spread.

- Cancer cells are dependent on a particular kind of energy metabolism and growing process comparable to that found in yeast.

- Cancer cells are highly resilient and adapt themselves to the surroundings and environment with every successive cell division.

- Cancer cells stimulate increased blood flow to themselves.

- Cancer cells attack local tissues and spread to other parts of the tissue and the body through the bloodstream.

- Cancer cells exchange genetic data with other cells in order to improve their own evolving capabilities.

It is not that every type of cancer cells will exhibit all the above traits; however, these strange characteristic features of cancer cells enhance the mystery and insidiousness of cancer cells. Genetic alterations are known to trigger these abnormal cell behaviors leading to increased proliferation of these cancer cells. The cancer cells invariably accumulate and form a lump referred to as a tumor or neoplasm. Tumors can be benign (non-spreading) or malignant (spreading).

Tumors that are benign are genetically or environmentally programmed to stop growing after a point in time and they do not spread to other tissues and/or organs. Contrarily, malignant tumors are formed from mutated cells that have the capability to stimulate the growth of blood vessels, feeding themselves more and more and increasing their evolving and growing capacity. These cells divert a lot more resources towards themselves and grow and expand to form a malignant tumor.

The good thing about the growth of cancer cells is the fact that they take years to mutate and the process has multiple and complex steps before the malignancy becomes a danger; therefore, it is possible to catch these cancer cells in the earlier stages. It is easier to treat cancers when they are caught early on as it is possible to stem their growth before they become strong and spread across the body. In fact, if caught early enough, it is possible to stop cancer at the cell level before the tumor is formed.

Causes of Cancer

It is nearly impossible to attribute one cause to the growth and spread of cancer cells because the formation process consists of multiple and complex steps and layers. Despite this, it has been observed in multiple experiments involving men and animals that many agents can initiate the growth and spread of cancer cells. These agents include different viruses, chemicals, and some forms of radiations.

Initiating Agents

The factors that trigger the initiation of cancer cells are called initiating agents. These agents damage DNA of cells in such a way that could potentially lead to cancerous mutations. A few of the initiating agents that are known to contribute to cancer in humans are:

- Ultraviolet radiation from the sun (this is the major cause of skin cancer).

- Ionizing radiation in the form of x-rays and radon.

- Carcinogenic chemicals from tobacco smoke (nearly 80-90% of lung and upper respiratory tract cancers are attributed to this).

- Carcinogenic chemicals from charred, smoked, or grilled meats.

- Some types of viruses (usually responsible for cervical carcinoma, liver cancer, and mitochondrial dysfunction).

- Aflatoxin (this is a very potent carcinogen that attacks the liver; it is usually produced by some molds contaminating peanuts and other grains that are stored improperly).

Tumor Promoters

There are many other components that can trigger cancer without causing DNA damage. These compounds are called tumor promoters because they cause an increased incidence of cell division; an important factor needed during the initial stages of tumor formation. Some hormones, such as estrogen, are known to be tumor promoters. The connection between estrogen and a tumor is the primary reason as to why women are more prone to the risk of cancer (especially breast cancer) than men. High levels of estrogen are also known to increase the risk of ovarian and endometrial cancers.

Obesity

While tumor promoters and initiating agents can trigger cancers, obesity is becoming an important reason for the onset of cancer. Obesity translates to excessive fat tissues in the body resulting in:

- Increased levels of chronic inflammation which causes damage to DNA and mitochondria in such a way that can trigger cancer.
- Increased production of estrogen, the tumor promoters.
- Increased levels of other growth promoters, such as IGF-1 and insulin.
- Impaired growth of healthy cells.

So, you can see that cancer is a highly complex disease with multiple causes and contributors. Yet, as more research is being conducted, it is becoming easier to understand and it is less mysterious than before;

however, there are multiple new traits being developed by cancer cells as they mutate, enhancing the level of complexity and complications.

One of the most important discoveries of treating cancer is by the way of dietary changes which have the power to decrease the risk of cancer and also improve the effectiveness of the treatment.

Metabolism and Cancer

One of the earliest observations made about cancer cells is that they depend primarily on glucose and glycolysis for their metabolism. These observations were made as early as the 1920s by Otto Warburg, the German scientist. In his study of cancer cells, Otto Warburg found that they convert a large amount of glucose into energy and lactic acid, a byproduct of glycolysis. This process is today referred to as the Warburg Effect.

Although today, genetic mutations are found to be one of the main causes of cancer. Altered energy metabolism is also a common biochemical feature shared by a majority of cancer cells. The Warburg Effect is an accepted hallmark of cancer cells.

Studies of molecular models and epidemiological studies show a strong connection between high levels of glucose in the bloodstream and the risk of cancer. Studies at the molecular level reveal that increased blood-glucose levels increase the growth of cancer cells, while deprivation of glucose leads to apoptosis or programmed cell death, resulting in reduced cancer cells.

It is a commonly acknowledged fact in the medical community that cancer cells are highly attracted to glucose; a fact that is used to get images of tumors. Lab technicians inject the patient's body with a glucose-based dye and use a machine to track its movement. The tumors in the body light up the maximum as the cancer cells strongly attract the glucose-based dye.

When people consume carb-rich diets, glucose becomes the body's primary fuel. Healthy cells and cancer cells manage the breakdown of glucose for energy differently. When healthy cells are at rest, they do not produce lactic acid. Contrarily, cancer cells break down glucose in a way that necessarily results in the production of lactic acid. This way of glucose breakdown results in the cells becoming increasingly vulnerable to genetic mutations. This, in turn, increases the toxicity of the cells with little or no hope of damage repair.

Like yeast, cancer cells gobble up available glucose and grow indiscriminately without any concern or care about the metabolic activities of neighboring healthy cells. Cancer cells become mutated to such an extent that they get converted to highly self-serving entities prepared to kill and attack anything that comes in their way of growth and expansion.

Mutated Mitochondria Syndrome and Therapy

Another important finding that throws light on the study of causes of cancer is the discovery of mutated and dysfunctional mitochondria; a component of the cell that is primarily responsible for the production of energy in the cell. When mitochondria become dysfunctional for a long period of time, a healthy cell can become a cancerous cell. If the cell is already cancerous, then dysfunctional mitochondria can enhance its vulnerability to additional cell mutations.

Consequently, these cancerous cells will become increasingly dependent on glucose to keep up the requirements of their yeast-like altered metabolism. This close connection between mitochondrial dysfunction, excessive dependence on glucose, and the growth of cancer cells, has led many researchers to think along the lines of a carbohydrate-restricted diet for cancer therapy.

This initial thought process has led to multiple studies that employed keto diets that restrict the availability of glucose to cancer cells as a form of complementary cancer therapy. It is therefore clear that a cancer patient on a keto diet is effectively cutting off the glucose supply to the cancer cells, thereby weakening their ability to grow and spread.

Scientific Research on Keto Diets in the Treatment of Cancer

The first study that observed the efficient use of a keto diet to treat cancer was published in 1995. In this study, two female cancer patients with Glioblastoma Multiforme (GBM), a particularly malignant form of cancer that originates in the brain and rapidly spreads to all the other parts of the body, were the subjects.

In addition to other conventional treatments, researchers advised the two patients to follow a ketogenic diet for 4 months. It was noticed that the blood-sugar levels in both the patients reduced to normal/low levels, and the ketone levels increased by nearly 20-30 times within seven days of following the prescribed keto diet.

Scan results also showed a 21.8% decrease in glucose uptake at the tumor areas in the brain for both the patients. A low glucose uptake in the area of a tumor reflects a shrinking tumor. One of the patients showed a considerable improvement in clinical health and continued the diet for a year after that. This patient exhibited nearly complete remission.

Another 65-year-old lady was taken as a subject in 2010. She was diagnosed with GBM and was prescribed a keto diet combined with water fasting and supplements for vitamins and minerals. Conventional medicinal treatments were also part of her cancer therapy; however, steroids were stopped. It was seen that after two months of this therapy, the brain tumor disappeared. A blood analysis revealed lowered glucose levels and increased ketone levels.

So, the above and many more case studies have revealed the efficacy of keto diets used in conjunction with conventional treatments in controlling cancer spreads. All the research work done on keto diets and cancer revealed that lowering glucose intake can potentially stem the growth of cancer.

Keto Diets with Intermittent Fasting as a Nutritional Therapy for Cancer

A better nutritional therapy than simply a keto diet is to combine it with intermittent fasting which drives the body to increase ketone levels from stored fatty acids to obtain energy for metabolism and other functions. With a regular supply of nutrition, the blood-sugar levels are always at a high, the insulin levels are at a high, and the fuel for the growth of cancer cells is never depleted. The modern-day diet consists of regular and frequent snacks and meals that ensure there is absolutely no shortage of glucose, making the environment highly conducive to cancer growth.

A good way to counter this is by combining keto diets with intermittent fasting which involves a period of 4-8 hours of eating duration and about 16-20 hours of fasting time. The fasting period compels the body to produce more ketones. This situation, combined with the lack of glucose, ensure cancer cells are not given much of a chance to survive and thrive.

Limitations of Keto Diets in the Treatment of Cancer

Now, in theory, if all the cancer cells thrive and grow by gorging on glucose, then a carb-restricted diet should have ideally been the ultimate and absolute cure for cancer. However, we must admit that this is not really true and that although keto diets have proven to be efficient complementary therapies for cancer, it cannot yet serve to reverse cancer formation completely and absolutely. The reason for this is the fact that there are other caveats of cancer that go beyond glucose needs.

First, not all cancer cells are made the same way. Each type of cancer cell follows its own set of survival and mutation mechanisms in order to grow, expand, and accumulate to form a tumor. For example, there could be cancer cells that grow and expand using substrates other than glucose. Recent studies have proven that cancer cells can thrive on a glutamine substrate as well. Glutamine is an amino acid obtained from protein-rich foods which are to be consumed while on a keto diet.

The second caveat is that proteins can be converted into glucose too and the third caveat is amino acids, such as leucine, can also stimulate the growth of cancer cells. Our body is designed in such a way that glucose is an essential ingredient for some metabolic activities. So, when you starve your body of carbs, it will find its own way to metabolize glucose from other non-carb substrates, such as fats and proteins, through a process referred to as gluconeogenesis. The glucose from non-carb substrates can also fuel cancer cell growth resulting in limiting the effectiveness of keto diets in the treatment of cancer.

Despite the above limitations, a keto diet is an effective way to limit the spread and growth of cancer cells considerably. Used in conjunction with other cancer treatments, keto diets are gaining in popularity to prevent and/or limit the risk of cancer. Restricting carbs is one of the best ways to improve mitochondrial function which, in turn, leads to improved cell health and reduced damage and prevention against genetic mutation.

So, it makes sense to include keto diet as part of your cancer treatment to improve chances of getting better.

Chapter 3: Critical Nutritional Therapeutic Information in a Well-Balanced Ketogenic Approach

Now that you understand why experts and researchers prescribe keto diets as a complementary therapy in the treatment of cancer, it makes sense to get right in and learn how you can build a keto diet for yourself. Before that, let us understand how the macro- and micronutrients are delivered to the body through a keto diet.

Nutrition from a keto diet should ideally be divided as follows:

- Fats
- 65-75% of your calories must come from fat sources.
- Proteins

- 15-30% of your calorific needs must be addressed by protein sources.
- Carbohydrates
- 5-10% of your calories must be from carbohydrates.

Fats

There is no way to gauge the amount of calories you need to consume through fat sources. You need not keep a tight count of calorie consumption from fats while on a keto diet because fatty foods keep you satiated for a longer time leaving you less frequently hungry than when you are on a carb-rich diet.

There are multiple studies that prove protein- and fat-rich foods are the most satiating foods, and carb-rich foods are the least satiating. Fats provide energy steadily to the body without causing insulin spikes, thereby reducing hunger pangs, cravings, and mood swings. When it comes to fats, it is more important to know the kinds of fats that are good for you and the kinds that are bad for you. The quality and type of fats used in your keto diet is more important than the amount of fat, although it is good to keep a check on the overall calorie intake and ensure it is within your daily limits.

Saturated Fats for Cooking

Until recently, saturated fats have been given a bad name owing to flawed research. Saturated fats have been wrongly blamed for causes of coronary and vascular diseases. However, there are numerous studies that have proved the earlier claims wrong.

Cooking in saturated fats is the most preferred way because of their high smoke points, their stable nature, and a long shelf life. Saturated fats are found primarily in cream, red meats, ghee, lard, butter, eggs, tallow, palm oil, and coconut oil. In keto diets, it is best if you get most of your fats in the form of saturated and/or mono-saturated fats.

Include Medium-Chain Triglycerides in Your Keto Diet

MCTs for short, medium-chain triglycerides, are found mostly in coconut oil. They can be easily ingested by the body. MCTs are directly sent to the liver in order to be used as an immediate source of energy, much like glucose. MCTs are also found in palm oil and butter, although to a much lesser degree.

Include Mono-Saturated Fatty Acids in Your Keto Diet

Found in nuts (especially macadamias), beef, olives, and avocados, mono-saturated fatty acids (MUFA, oleic acid, and omega-9) are known to prevent coronary diseases. Consumption of this form of fatty acids is known to be connected with improved serum-lipid profiles. MUFA-rich oils such as olive oil, macadamia nut oil, and avocado oil, are best for use in their cold forms for finishing a dish or drizzling after the cooking process.

Use Unsaturated Fats without Heating

Polyunsaturated fatty acids (PUFA), omega-6 and omega-3 fatty acids are essential for the human body, yet our diets are mostly rich in PUFA and, therefore, needs to be regulated. The name 'poly' in PUFA refers to the presence of multiple double bonds.

On heating, these double bonds react with oxygen to produce free radicals. The oxidative process causes inflammation and increases the risk of heart diseases and cancer. It is recommended that PUFA should not exceed 4% of your daily calorific needs. PUFA oils, such as oils from nuts, flaxseed, sesame, and avocado, should be used in the cold. In fact, flaxseed oil should always be refrigerated. The other oils can be used for light cooking only.

Important Elements of Fats

The three most important elements to focus on before choosing your fats is shelf life, smoke point, and oxidation rate. The higher the smoke point of a fat, the better it is for you. Oils with high smoke points can be cooked at high temperatures, ensuring that the oil and the nutrients are not damaged in the heating process. Moreover, oils with high smoke points do not react with oxygen during the heating process to create harmful free radicals.

The slower the oxidation rate, the better the oil. It is important to use oils with slow oxidation rates. While it is natural for oxidation rates to increase on heating as the temperate nears their smoking points, there are many oils and fats that oxidize even in the cold when exposed to light, oxygen, and moisture, even at temperatures below the smoking point.

Oils with a low shelf life can turn rancid which increases the level of free radicals in them. In general, oils with a high density of saturated fats have a longer shelf life than those with a low density of saturated fats.

Avoid Unhealthy Oils

These include margarine, processed vegetable oils, partially and fully hydrogenated oils, etc which can damage your health. Avoid trans-fatty acids as well.

Tips to Include More Healthy Fats for Nutritional Therapy

Flavorful, full-fat ingredients are highly satisfying meals that can keep your hunger at bay for a long time. Moreover, you already know how useful healthy fats are to fight off cancer. Despite the advantage, converting your diet to a primarily fat-based one can be quite challenging so here are some excellent tips for it.

Use Only Full-Fat and Whole Ingredients

Take away all low-fat and no-fat ingredients from your cupboard and refrigerator. Remove all egg-beaters, artificial creamers, low-fat peanut butter, and anything that says low-fat or no-fat. Include fat-rich ingredients like avocados, butter, ghee, full-fat yogurt, heavy cream, etc into your grocery list. Buy fatty cuts of meat instead of lean meat. They are more flavorful and cheaper as well. Include sardines and salmon into your refrigerator stock.

Cook with Healthy Fats

Avoid steaming your foods while on a keto diet. Fry them in healthy natural fats, such as butter, ghee and coconut oil. Use as much fat as you need. Don't scrimp at all.

Use a Variety of Fats to Get a Variety of Flavors

Fats can alter the taste of a dish. For example, a slather of butter on top of a crispy vegetable salad can change it into a comfort food to die for. Sauté your meats and vegetables in peanut oil, or drizzle olive oil or sesame oil for a different flavor. Make sure you have the following fats in your larder:

- Butter

- Tallow, lard, duck fat, and other animal-based fats
- Coconut oil
- Avocado oil
- Olive oil
- Peanut oil
- Oils from other nuts such as macadamia, almonds, and walnuts
- Sesame oil

Top All Dishes with Oil, Dressing, or Butter

Pour healthy and natural forms of fats and oils on dressing, drizzle them on salads, spread them on meat dishes, spoon them into soups and other dishes, ladle them into flourless chili and sauces, and more. Put a dollop of whipped heavy cream over your macadamia nut flour waffles. Blend heavy cream into tea and coffee.

Proteins

Proteins are the building blocks of all tissues and are essential nutrients for our body. Proteins can also be used as a source of fuel. At this juncture, it might be a good idea to clarify that keto diets are not protein-rich diets. They are high in fat content, moderate in protein content, and low on carbs.

The reason for proteins to be included in moderation in a keto diet is the fact that excessive proteins can trigger your body out of ketosis. Consumption of too little proteins is also not good for the body as it could lead to weak muscles and increased appetite. In addition to being a very satisfying food source (which prevents frequent hunger and cravings), proteins are also known to increase energy expenditure. This means proteins drive the body to burn more calories.

How Much Protein to Consume?

The amount of protein needed by the body is dependent on the body weight and the amount of physical activity. It means that physically active people need more proteins than those who lead a sedentary lifestyle. You can calculate the amount of protein needed by your body by arriving at the lean mass which is obtained by subtracted body fat from the total body weight.

The amount of proteins you need can be arrived using the following simple formulae as well:

- Body weight (in pounds) multiplied by 0.6 and 1 (to get the minimum and maximum protein intake per day).
- Body weight (in kilograms) multiplied by 1.3 and 2.2 (for minimum and maximum).

Other factors that affect the amount of proteins needed are gender and age. Consuming sufficient amounts of protein is essential to build and maintain healthy muscle mass. However, while on a keto diet, it is important to remember not to consume excessive protein as it can throw your body out of ketosis which is the primary and final aim of a keto diet. Excessive proteins in your system can compel your body to use them as a source of fuel instead of ketones, thereby preventing your body from going into ketosis. Of course, this happens only when a significant amount of proteins are consumed. A few extra grams will not make a difference.

Carbohydrates

To be able to enter ketosis, you must restrict the amount of carbs you consume. There are two ways you can use to find the ideal carb intake required for you to enter ketosis.

Low to High Level

In this method, you start your keto diet with a very low amount of carbs (not more than 20 gm of net carbs each day). This will allow your body to quickly get into a state of ketosis. After a couple of days, your body will get into ketosis. At this point, start adding carbs in your daily diet by about 5 gm a week until you find very low levels of, or no ketones, in your body. Keeping a blood ketone meter handy is good when you are starting off on a keto diet.

This method is the most reliable method of finding the net carbohydrate limit of your body. It might be a little difficult, especially during the initial couple of days when you will be required to give up all forms of carbs until ketosis sets in. However, it will be worth your while because you will get an accurate number of your body's net carb limit.

High to Low Level

As you will not be in ketosis when you start off your keto diet, you can start with a high level of carb intake per day and keep reducing it by about 5 gm each week until you detect ketones in your body. This is an easier approach than the previous one and yet is not recommended because your body will be out of ketosis for a very long time before you find the correct net carb limit.

An important point to remember at this stage is that it takes a couple of days for your body to completely deplete glucose before getting into ketosis so, if there is a delay in the onset of ketosis, simply wait patiently. The work is happening at an unseen level and it will take time for results to become obvious.

Micronutrients

It is a natural thing to feel the panic of missing out on certain vital nutrients when you start off on any diet, especially keto diets, wherein a large number of ingredients and foods have to be eliminated from your diet. The fear of risk of micronutrient deficiency in such a scenario is natural, expected, and good for you because it means you are not doing the diet as a fad but with all your faculties working right.

The Importance of Tracking Micronutrients in Keto Diets

A low-carb keto diet can be perfect to achieve all your micronutrient needs, providing you are thinking through the diet planning process in the right way. If you focus excessively on keto macros by going overboard with bacon and butter and forget to look at micronutrients, then micronutrient deficiencies are bound to hit you hard.

Cancer patients are especially prone to micronutrient deficiency as is evident from many cancer diagnoses which also reveal these deficiencies. Moreover, the level of micronutrients is negatively impacted when cancer therapy starts and, therefore, it is imperative to include foods rich in all the essential micronutrients in your keto diet.

The best way to ensure you get sufficient amounts of micronutrients in your keto diet is by including a lot of vegetables in your meals. Here are some common micronutrient deficiencies that can occur by an ineffective keto diet focused too much on macros.

Sodium

Keto diets can create a diuretic situation in your body driven by the elimination of carbs. This means once your body gets into ketosis, it will begin to eliminate a lot of water, along with plenty of essential micronutrients in general, and sodium in particular. It is important to keep track of this essential micronutrient and limit sodium loss through compensation.

The symptoms of low sodium include extreme fatigue, headaches, and the inability to do strenuous work. Your keto diet, in the initial days, must include sodium in the range of 3000 to 5000 mg per day. Consuming bone broth or bouillon and adding a little extra salt in your food will help you achieve this.

Potassium

Sodium loss is invariably accompanied by a loss of potassium too. Potassium deficiency symptoms include physical weakness, irritability, constipation, skin problems, and reduced muscle mass. About 4500 mg of daily potassium is needed while on a keto diet. Potassium-rich keto foods include mushrooms, kale, avocado, and spinach.

Magnesium

is used in over 300 biochemical reactions in the human body and plays a very important role in energy production, protein synthesis, cell reproduction, and fatty acid formation. Symptoms of magnesium deficiency include muscle cramps, fatigue, and dizziness. On a keto diet, you need about 500 mg of magnesium per day. Magnesium-rich foods include oysters, pumpkin seeds, Swiss chard, and spinach.

Calcium

An important micronutrient for the health of bones and teeth; calcium is also needed for:

- Blood clotting
- Transmitting signals between nerves
- Regulating blood pressure

Despite calcium being available in plentiful in our bones, it is essential to consume calcium every day to prevent deficiencies. In the initial stages of keto diets, calcium is flushed out along with many other electrolytes and it is important to replace the loss. You need to consume about 1000-2000 mg per day while on a keto diet. Calcium-rich foods include almonds, broccoli, kale, and sardines.

B Vitamins

As keto diets include a lot of dark green leafy vegetables, the concern for B vitamins deficiency is not relevant.

In addition to the above micronutrients, it is essential to include iron, iodine, phosphorus, zinc, and all other Vitamins in your keto diet.

Chapter 4: Individualized Keto-Based Dietary Therapies

Getting the right keto diet, especially when you are starting off, can appear to be a daunting task. Add to that, the woes of cancer therapies can easily put off the most courageous person from making the attempt to make suitable changes to his or her diet. That is the reason why this chapter is included in this book.

The recommendations below will give you an idea of what foods you should replace, along with replacement options. This detailed information will help you sustain your keto diets for a long time without worrying about what to eat and what not to eat. This list will help you make viable customizations of your keto diet, and give you sufficient room to make changes regularly so as to keep monotony at bay.

Tips to Start Off

Getting your body to enter ketosis quickly is an effective way to ensure you remain motivated. The success of a quick ketosis will drive you to work harder. Here are some quick tips to enter the ketosis mode quickly:

- Stop eating out for some time.
- Cook your own foods to control your carb intake.
- Make sure you track your ingredients with a microscope to ensure you are not missing out on hidden carbs.
- Drink plenty of water.
- Avoid processed foods altogether (for some time, at least).
- Understand and accept the fact there is no magic to fixing any problem. It requires hard work, patience, and courage. Keto for healing is specifically harder than for weight loss and it

is essential that you speak to your physician before arriving at a diet that is suitable for your needs.

- Keto diets do not focus on counting calories; instead, they focus on the quality of food you consume.

- Never stop asking questions and do a lot of research to find answers.

- Be wary of people who discourage your efforts. Stay away from them and surround yourself with motivators and positive-thinking people.

Breakfast Replacements

Generally, a simple keto diet has bacon and eggs for breakfast. Although it is a great meal, it might get repetitive and may not hit the occasional cravings of the body.

- Replace milk-based yogurt (flavored or plain) with full fat Greek yogurt, coconut milk yogurt, full fat cottage cheese, and sour cream.

- Replace cereals with pork rind cereal, flax granola, chia pudding, and toasted nuts.

- Replace oatmeal with cauliflower, cinnamon roll oatmeal, flaxseed oatmeal, and chia seeds.

- Replace waffles and pancakes with cream cheese pancakes, peanut butter pancakes, blueberry ricotta pancakes, keto pumpkin pancakes, peanut pancakes, and almond flour pancakes.

- Replace egg whites with whole eggs; it is important to include fat-rich foods that come with rich flavors as well. You can eat whole eggs in any form including boiled, scrambled, deviled eggs, egg salad, or egg benedict.

Lunch and Snack Replacements

Lunch is usually a simple affair for a person on a keto diet. It could be leftovers from the dinner of the previous day, or a simple salad using meats, greens, and homemade dressings. Here are some great replacements for lunch and snack items while on a keto diet.

Replace sandwiches and bread with flax seed and/or lettuce wraps. You can have cabbage rolls or lettuce rolls filled with your favorite meats fried in an MCT oil of your choice. A psyllium husk or a flax seed wrap is a great replacement too.

Replace your cookies and chips with dehydrated veggies or low-carb cookies. You can invest in a dehydrator for domestic use and cut thin strips of your favorite vegetables and dehydrate them for 12 hours. Your healthy, keto-friendly chips are ready to snack or include as a side item in your lunch. At your local grocery store or on any online store, you can find a lot of keto-friendly low-carb cookies too.

Replace your dips and crackers with chia seed and flax seed crackers. Easy to make chia seed, almond flour, and flax seed crackers will hit the craving for crunch at the right spot.

Replace all kinds of sweets with mug cakes and fat bombs. Mug cakes are a perfect replacement and will hit your sweet craving. You should avoid all kinds of sweets including sugar, honey, etc. Use stevia, allulose, monk fruit, and erythritol instead.

Stevia is a natural sweetener extracted from a plant of the same name belonging to the marigold family. Two glycosides found in stevia, including rebaudioside and stevioside, are responsible for the sweetness. It is a great low-carb substitute for sugar and is recommended for use in keto diets.

Allulose is a monosaccharide (or single sugar) and its anti-fermenting ability creates fewer gut issues such as gas, cramping, or bloating. With a glycemic index of zero, allulose produces zero blood-insulin or blood-sugar spikes, thereby making it a perfect sugar replacement in keto diets. Allulose is, however, very difficult to find in foods and only a few very natural ingredients, such as raisins, figs and wheat contain this low-carb sugar.

Monk fruit is another natural sweetener available today. It contains mogrosides and has zero calories with a sweetness level that is 400 times that of cane sugar. Mogrosides are metabolized by our body in such a way that there are no spikes in blood-sugar and blood-insulin levels.

Erythritol is very popular in keto diets owing to its low carb levels. This honey-based sugar substitute adds a sweet taste to your dishes without the associated carbs and calories.

Dinner Replacements

A balanced keto dinner would include a moderate amount of protein with added fat and a dish of dark, green leafy salad with added fat. Yet, keto diets offer sufficient room to help you find dinner options when you are looking for a heavy meal to manage those cravings.

Replace fries and burgers with buttered broccoli and buttered steak with a salad dish. A medium steak portion slathered with butter will help you manage your craving for burgers and fries. Also, you can try creamy cheese spinach casserole.

Replace pizzas with dough made with mozzarella cheese and almond flour. Pizza crust made with this combination is perfect for that thin, crispy pizza-eating feel.

Replace fried chicken with pork rind and parmesan crust. Replace processed soups with heavy-cream-based soups. You can make keto-friendly soups using sausages, kale, spinach, bacon, cauliflower, broccoli, and more. Feel free to add fresh cream for that keto rush. These soups will fill you on your protein needs, and also your fat needs, while keeping you hunger-free for a long time.

Replace pasta with shirataki and zucchini noodles. Also called as zoodles, zucchini noodles can be a satisfying keto-friendly replacement for pasta cravings. There are spiralizers available in the market to help you get that perfectly shaped zoodles.

Replace rice with cauliflower rice and make delicious fried rice with your favorite meat pieces, scrambled eggs, and crunchy vegetables too. You can also mash cauliflower to mimic mashed potatoes. Replace tacos and burritos with flax and psyllium husk tortillas.

Beverage Replacements

Water is the go-to drink in keto diets. Replace juices and sodas with no-sugar drinks. Replace fruit juices with tea and low-carb smoothies. Tea is available in a variety of flavors that can be easily taken in place of water right through the day. Smoothie options include peanut butter smoothie, cucumber-spinach smoothie, blackberry-chocolate smoothie, etc.

Replace coffee and sugar with coffee and stevia. You can include a heavy whipping cream to your coffee if you are used to creamy coffee. Replace milk and coffee creamer with coconut or almond milk.

You can replace your frappes and cappuccinos with coffee made with coconut oil and butter instead of milk or generic cream.

Replace cocktails with liquor and dry wine. Liquor, with nearly zero carbs, is the best choice, followed by dry wines which have about 3-5g of carbs per glass.

Make sure you identify and keep out flavored and mixed liquors as they are bound to have hidden carbs. Replace all your liquor mixers and chasers with lemon, water, and diet soda. The only time you can make an exception of diet soda (while on a keto diet) is while drinking.

Alcohol and Cancer

At this juncture, as this book is more to do with cancer and keto rather than anything else, a word of caution against alcohol is appropriate. Multiple studies have revealed a deep connection between alcohol use and cancer, especially cancers of the mouth, larynx, throat, esophagus, liver, colon, rectum, and breast. Therefore, a keto diet for cancer should necessarily eliminate the use of alcohol completely. Speak to your physician and make an informed choice about alcohol.

So, you can see that there are plenty of options and replacement foods available to fit a keto diet that is sustainable in the long run. The initial days might be a little struggle as you engage in trial and error methods to find replacements that suit your lifestyle, your palate, and the healing process you have undertaken. Like all medical-based concepts, it is best to discuss your keto diet with your oncologist and make sure you are getting optimum results.

Chapter 5: Ketogenic Cooking Techniques and Dining Out

Keto diets have a different approach from the usual when it comes to cooking techniques. This chapter is dedicated to giving you the cooking techniques that are best for keto dishes, and also what to look out for when you choose to dine out.

The Gram Scale

The gram scale is an essential tool that will be needed in the kitchen as you prepare yourself to begin your keto diet. It is best to invest in a gram scale that weighs a minimum of 1000g, although a 2000g scale would be ideal. Ensure you make the scale reading to zero with the container before you put in the ingredients that need to be measured. The rule of thumb to weigh wet ingredients is to ensure that it is not more or less than 0.3g of the required amount.

Heavy Cream

Heavy cream is a very important ingredient in your keto diet. When you buy heavy cream, ensure the following:

- Expiry date is a long way away.
- Fat content is at least 5-6g.
- Carbs and protein content should both be zero.
- Avoid buying heavy creams with additives too.

You can whip heavy cream using any kind of blender or hand mixer. Once whipped, you can store the cream in an airtight container in the refrigerator. Weigh the cream only after you have whipped it for greater accuracy.

Egg Whites

It is best to whip eggs when they are completely chilled. They whip faster and better when eggs are cold. It is good to use a high-sided clean bowl to whip egg whites as they will tend to scatter less than in a low-sided bowl. Separate the egg whites from the yolk. You can whip the egg whites with a simple hand blender until you reach the stiff peak stage. This is when the peaks of the whipped egg whites stand stiff on the blender. Egg whites are great to put into your keto-friendly dishes for added fluffiness and texture and to meet the moderate protein requirements.

Flour and Nut Butter

Using homemade flour and nut butter is an excellent option for keto diets to ensure that there are no hidden ingredients adding unnecessarily carb value to your foods (a common problem when you choose to buy nut butter from the store). Here is how to make almond butter.

Add two cups of unsalted and unroasted almonds to a food processor. Run the processor until the nuts are pulverized to the texture of coarse sand. Make sure there are no large pieces of almonds in this mixture. You now have homemade almond meal ready. At this stage, you must continue to run the food processor at high speeds until the almond gets converted to almond butter. You will have to mix the almond mixture several times during this process to ensure all the dry pieces of almonds are getting pulverized too. Continue grinding until you get a smooth and sticky almond butter.

The same process can be used to make macadamia nut butter with unroasted and unsalted macadamia nuts. Macadamia nut butter is easier to make because of its higher fat content as compared to almonds. The tastelessness of macadamia nuts makes the butter perfect for use in keto diets.

To make macadamia nut flour, you can use a rotary cheese grater. Macadamia nut flour is perfect to make waffles for your keto breakfast, or you can use macadamia nut butter too. Just add some eggs, macadamia nut flour, and some frozen blueberries (for added sweetness) and your keto waffle dough is ready.

Low Carb Cooking

The primary goal of a ketogenic diet is to focus on homemade dishes using fresh, local ingredients. Every meal should consist of a protein in the form of seafood, meat, or poultry that is cooked in natural MCT oils, along with low-carb vegetables on the side. All dressings and sauces have to be made with natural fats and oils with spices of your choice.

The trick in keto-friendly foods is to keep carb intake at very low levels. Starch and sugars have to be completely avoided. These foods include grains and their flours, bread, crackers, starchy veggies, such as peas and potatoes, and sweeteners like cornstarch and sugar. Here are some illustrations of keto-friendly low carb cooking:

Chili and stews are generally made by smothering the meats with flour. In a keto-friendly dish, you must leave out the flour in the cooking process and at the end, you should add some low-carb vegetable puree for thickening. You can cook meats, seafood, and poultry by grilling, roasting, sautéing, baking, poaching, broiling, and steaming. Just remember not to add any flours in the cooking process.

Natural fats like butter are the best to use in keto dishes. It can be used to bake, grill, sauté, and fry meats and low-carb vegetables. Butter is great to make sauces or to include in baked dishes or to use as a spread. Butter is good only for low-heat frying. Olive oil is another good choice for low heat frying of keto dishes.

To make it convenient for keto cooking, ensure the following:

- Stock up your cupboard and refrigerators with keto-friendly ingredients.

- Make extra servings so that you can use them for another meal or two.

- Keep a meat temperature chart and oil temperature chart handy.

- Don't scrimp on investing in useful cooking devices and utensils to turn out keto foods in convenient and easy ways.

- Never stop learning new recipes.

Dining Out for Keto Dieters

Just because you have chosen to change your dietary status in an effort to heal yourself, doesn't mean you cannot go out and have a bit of fun. Dining out is one of the most popular ways to socialize in the modern world. Moreover, when you are down in the dumps, dining out with family and friends can lift your spirits like nothing else. Being on a keto diet, you simply need to be extra wary of the dishes you choose to eat while dining out. Here are some tips:

Keep out the starch. Don't order bread, pasta, potatoes, rice, and sweets too. Many restaurants are now keto-friendly and will help with the following:

- They are willing to substitute extra veggies or salads in place of entrees.
- They will replace the burgers with lettuce wraps.

If the restaurant cannot replace the required ingredients, you simply ensure that you don't eat the starchy items on the dish.

Add healthy fat. Most of the restaurant meals lack in healthy fat leaving you feeling very unsatisfied, especially in the absence of starch and sugars, but you can fix it by asking for:

- Extra butter and melt on the meats and vegetables.
- Extra olive oil and drizzle liberally over salads and the main course.

Many restaurants replace good, healthy oils with cheap oils that defeat the purpose of a keto diet. If you are unsure of the quality of food in the restaurant, you should definitely carry a small bottle of olive oil and/or butter with you.

Watch out for sauces. Some sauces have healthy keto-friendly butter and olive oil in them; however, many of the sauces and dressings are filled with carbs. Always ask for the sauce on the side. You can check out what it contains and then choose to include it or eliminate it. Leave out ketchup because they contain a lot of carbs. If you choose mustard, ensure it is a sugar-free one such as Dijon mustard. Avoid barbeque sauces because they are filled with carbs.

Get creative if there is nothing available for your keto needs. If there is a Spaghetti Bolognese dish, ask for the sauce only in a soup bowl along with a green leafy vegetable salad on the side. Sprinkle some parmesan cheese on the soup and the salad for that added fat.

If you are dining at a buffet restaurant, focus on the following tips:

- Use a small plate to ensure you don't overeat, even if it is starch and sugar.
- Focus on proteins, vegetables, and fats.
- Use the seafood spread, food from the carving stations, and vegetable platters are the best.
- Remember to add healthy fats like sour cream, butter, cheese, and olive oil to your plate.

- Don't eat in a hurry.

- Eat slowly, ensuring you chew every mouthful mindfully. Enjoy the conversation at the table too.

- Gulp down water and slowly sip alcohol.

Don't let a keto diet stop you from having fun with family and friends. Keep an open mind and be willing to make sacrifices in the interest of your own health.

Chapter 6: Other Factors Integrated with Keto Diets for Effective Metabolic Therapy

There are hardly any diseases that can be countered with a single-pronged approach, especially complex ones such as cancer. A multi-pronged approach is needed to stem the spread of the ugly disease. This chapter is dedicated to other factors that need to be integrated into a keto diet in order to effectively fight off cancer on the basis of nutritional metabolism.

Exercise

Regular exercise is an imperative aspect of any healing process, and it is true for cancer treatments as well. Regular exercises help cancer patients in the following way:

- Maintains and improves physical well-being.

- Improves overall physical balance and reduces risks of bone breakages and falls.
- Keep muscles active and prevents them from being wasted due to inactivity.
- Lowers the risk of heart diseases.
- Improves blood flow to limbs.
- Reduces the risk of depression and anxiety.
- Reduces symptoms of fatigue.
- Improves the quality of life and helps to keep weight gain in check.

The following things have to be considered when you talk to your trainer to set up a regular exercise regimen:

- The stage and type of cancer.
- The treatment being followed.
- The diet.
- Fitness and endurance levels.

In a keto diet, restricting carbs limits the access of sugar, the fastest energy fuel, to muscles. With reduced access to sugar-based energy, initially, it is possible that your ability to do high-intensity exercises is impaired; therefore, it is important to let your doctor and trainer know about your keto diet so that they can strategize the best training regimen for you.

Moreover, while exercising on a keto diet, it is imperative that you get the right and recommended quantities of proteins and fats to prevent any mishap.

Alcohol Consumption

Alcohol is best avoided if you are using keto diets to fight against cancer as there is a clear connection between the causes of cancer and alcohol use. Yet, for the sake of academics, the following tips can be kept in mind while on a keto diet:

Wine

You can, perhaps, have a glass of dry wine (less than 20 gm a day) while on a keto diet. Dry wines contain nearly negligible amounts of insulin-spiking sugars and, therefore, are great accompaniments to a keto-friendly meal. Dessert wines, on the other hand, are to be avoided as they contain a lot more sugar than is recommended in a keto diet.

Beer

is a huge problem for keto diets. There are a lot of sugars with a high glycemic index that can harm the purpose of a keto diet while providing a conducive sugar-filled atmosphere for cancer cells to survive and thrive.

Other alcoholic drinks

Pure spirits such as brandy, whiskey, vodka, cognac, and tequila contain zero carbs and are good for use in keto; however, cocktails, which are usually sweetened drinks, are to be avoided. The highly popular gin and tonic is full of sugar and a complete no-no for keto diets. A simple drink of vodka, lime, and soda water is a fabulous alternative. The worst thing to do with alcohol is to mix it with juice and soda which is nothing but a big sugar bomb to be completely avoided.

The top alcoholic drinks that are keto-friendly include:

1. Dry sparkling wine or champagne

Whether it is the expensive French variety or the more affordable options in your local supermarket, dry sparkling wines contain less than 1g of carbs and are great for keto diets.

2. Dry wine

With only about 2g of carbs, dry wines can be consumed while on a keto diet.

3. Whiskey

With nearly zero carbs, this pure spirit is a great accompaniment for a keto-friendly meal.

4. Dry Martini

Vodka, vermouth, and lime combine well, giving you a zero-carb alcoholic keto-friendly drink.

An important element to remember is that people on keto diets need little alcohol to get high; therefore, it is possible to save money and keep your blood-glucose at respectable levels while drinking on a keto diet. For cancer-diagnosed patients, it is very, very important to speak to your physician before you drink alcohol of any kind.

Managing Keto Diets on Sick Days

Being sick can make it easy for anyone to fall out of a well-established keto diet. Use these tips and endeavor at your attempts and you will come through unscathed.

Hydrate

Getting dehydrated when you are sick is a common thing to happen. Symptoms of dehydration are dry lips, dry eyes, and decreased urine output. You must drink a lot more water and consume a lot more beverages to remain hydrated. Try and have at least one cup of fluid every hour to prevent becoming dehydrated. Any calorie-free beverage or water will work wonders.

Maintain the diet if it is possible

If the diet is tolerated by your body, then keep maintaining it. However, if nausea, vomiting, and diarrhea are creating problems, then you can shift to reduced calorie meals temporarily and get back as soon as you feel fine. Moreover, during the sick days, it is fine to lower ketone levels and replace with glucose which is essential for fighting infections. It is not difficult to get back to ketosis after this temporary break.

Check out any new medications you have been prescribed

This is especially important if you are being treated for cancer. New medications could be interfering with old ones and causing problems. Do check with your physician if the symptoms persist.

Avoid getting into excessive ketosis

If your body is not being able to tolerate foods over a considerably long period of time, it is possible for your body to get into excessive ketosis. Symptoms of this state include fussiness, rapid breathing, excessive fatigue, facial flushing, and nausea.

When you are sick, it is important to listen to your body and heed its warnings. If needed, do not hesitate to cut back on the diet and get back after you are feeling better.

Supplements on a Keto Diet

It is important to include supplements in your keto diet because it alters the way your metabolism works. Until now, your body has been used to churning glucose for energy, and when you deprive it of its primary source of fuel, it is going to react and change gears. Like all changes, this shift is also going to be painful and a lot of adjustment will be needed before your body settles down to ketosis. During this time, supplements are helpful in this following ways:

- They reduce the discomforts associated with keto flu often set off by the lack of vitamins and minerals as the body begins the transition to ketosis.

- They fill in nutritional gaps in keto diets.

- They optimize results for which the keto diet was started, such as healing diseases, weight loss, and fat loss.

The important supplements to include in your keto diet are:

Electrolytes

Of which sodium, magnesium, potassium, and calcium are the most important ones for smooth metabolism.

Vitamin D

This is a vital nutrient for healthy hormones and strength. Vitamin D is produced by the body in the presence of sunlight so if you live in a place with little sunlight, you could be deficient in this vitamin. When you are on a keto diet for healing cancer (which is already a compromised health status), it is better to be well-equipped with all the nutrients needed for the smooth functioning of your body. Moreover, excessive exposure to sunlight can also cause skin cancer.

Other than the above, depending on your lifestyle, course of treatment, and needs, you can include other supplements such as spirulina (for lowered cholesterol), chlorella (to fight fatigue), bone broth (an excellent supplement for all electrolytes), dandelion roots (for improved fat absorption), turmeric (an excellent anti-inflammatory), and more.

Conclusion

It has been proven time and again that a healthy diet made with natural foods is an effective complementary therapy to contain and, even, eliminate cancer from your body. Even if the research is not absolutely clear on the validity of a keto diet in being a great cure for cancer, there is no doubt that a healthy diet is the cornerstone of a healthy quality of life.

Wholesome natural foods will drive the growth of healthy cells and tissues, thereby reducing the chances of genetic mutation, the primary origin of cancer cells. Here is a summary of the proven strategies that are effective combatants against cancer (in addition to the conventional cancer treatments):

- A well-balanced keto diet complemented with intermittent fasting.
- A calorie-restricted diet for weight management.

- A carb-restricted diet to reduce the chances of the survival of cancer cells.

- Ample exercises that are aligned with the patient's lifestyle and needs.

- Supplements to counter micronutrient deficiencies.

- Restriction or elimination of alcohol consumption.

In addition to the above, it is important to lead a stress-free life with sufficient sleep. Medical professionals recommend stress release by indulging in hobbies, meditation, and other stress-releasing activities.

Managing and combating cancer is not a simple process. It is as complex and layered as the mind-boggling number of possible causes for its origin. Cancer treatments are usually multipronged and require therapies to be administered from various quarters in addition to the conventional medical treatments. An effective carb-restricted diet, like the keto diet, is a great way to complement other treatment methods.

Thank you for Buying this Book.

May I take this opportunity to thank you for purchasing this book. I would love to hear your opinion on this book and I am pleased that you have selected our company and bought this informative book. Please, check out other books in our collection, spanning different topics to be informed on health and fitness trends.

Made in the USA
Middletown, DE
19 December 2018